THE EARLY CHURCH
FROM CHRIST TO CONSTANTINE

by

Fr Anthony Meredith SJ

*All booklets are published thanks to the
generous support of the members of the
Catholic Truth Society*

CATHOLIC TRUTH SOCIETY
PUBLISHERS TO THE HOLY SEE

Contents

Introduction

On 22nd May AD 337, the emperor Constantine lay dying at Nicomedia in Bithynia, a Roman province to the north west of Turkey, not far from modern Istanbul. Shortly before his death, he had been baptised by the bishop of the city, Eusebius. He was buried together with the supposed remains of the twelve apostles, in the Church of the Holy Apostles, in an attempt to symbolically have him looked upon by posterity as the thirteenth apostle. His conversion to Christianity may perhaps have taken place about 25 years previously, shortly before the battle of the Milvian Bridge on 28th October 312. At that battle, which is described for us by Eusebius in book 9, chapter 9 of his *Ecclesiastical History* he had beaten his rival and co emperor, Maxentius. We are also told by Lactantius (c.250-325) in his *On the deaths of Persecutors,* 44 that the emperor had seen the chi rho sign in the sky, XP the first two letters of the Greek word for Christ, and underneath the words "In this sign conquer". This monogram Constantine had placed on the shields of his troops and to this he attributed his victory.

Freedom of worship

In 313 Constantine having established a temporary
alliance with Licinius, to whom his sister Constantia had
been married, issued together with him, a rescript usually
(and inaccurately) described as 'The Edict of Milan',
which granted freedom of worship to all, including
Christians. Eusebius in his *Ecclesiastical History* (10, 5,
7) records the rescript as follows: "We have granted to
these same Christians free and unrestricted authority to
observe their own form of worship". A similar version in
Latin of the celebrated rescript is preserved by Lactantius
in chapter 48 of the above mentioned work.

He completed his design of uniting the whole of the
empire under himself by defeating his former ally,
Licinius, ruler of the eastern part of the empire at the
battle of Chrysopolis in 324. Though initially
pardoned he was subsequently strangled in mid 325.
On 12th May 330 Constantine transferred the capital
of the empire from Rome to Constantinople, a move
which effectively divided the empire into two halves,
east and west and helps explain the differences
between divided Christendom, which are still with us
today. The dividing line was in the Balkans and the
present religious differences between Orthodox
Serbia, and Roman Catholic Croatia reflect that
ancient division.

Constantine's conversion

The actual motives for the 'conversion' of Constantine are hard for us to unravel. Two grounds, in particular, have been alleged for his change of heart. The first and inevitably for many the preferred is political. The emperor was shrewd enough to perceive two things. The first was that the part of the empire, the western part, which he had inherited from his father, Constantius on his death in 306, was becoming increasingly Christian. About a tenth of its population, if that, had embraced the gospel by that time. The second was that traditional paganism was in a state of terminal decline. The second motive advanced was that of religious conviction. the worship of the unconquered sun, which owed much to the Emperor Aurelian (270-275) had much in common with the gospel and it needs to be remembered that Helena, the emperor's mother was a devout Christian. On balance the former arguments seem more persuasive, despite the interesting suggestion of Robin Lane Fox that paganism was not quite so decrepit as is often thought.

In any event, with the help of the God of the Christians he had been victorious, and in thanksgiving had in the following year, 313, issued, as we have seen the 'Edict of Milan'. By this Christians were able to hold property and worship publicly and their bishops were entitled to use the imperial postal service. This momentous event turned the Christians, at best a strong minority, into a tolerated and increasingly influential body within the empire. They were soon to become even more favoured, and with a slight interruption, during the brief reign of Julian the Apostate (361-363) the Christian Church continued to enjoy great favour for the next 1500 years. This increase in power and influence may well have diluted the purity of motive of those who espoused the Christian religion.

Mixed blessing

It is important to remember two things about this event. i) It did not take place in a vacuum; ii) it was a mixed blessing:

i) By the time Constantine's conversion took place in 312, the Church had already acquired many of the features she still possesses. As early as AD 200 she had spread as far south as India and as far west as Britain, there were already three British bishops present at the council of Arles in 314. The Church already possessed a structured hierarchy of bishop, priest and deacon; she also possessed a canon or list of recognised New Testament scriptures and was on the threshold of formulating her basic convictions about the person of Christ in the Creed at the Council of Nicaea which opened on 19th June 325.

ii) There were great blessings for the Church in state patronage; freedom from persecution being the most important and the ability to worship publicly. There were, however, certain attendant dangers. Emperors liked to have a co-operative, if not a subservient church, in return for obvious blessings. Conformity, therefore, became a valued virtue. Instead of the disadvantages, which often accompanied conversion, it now came to be seen as an opportunity for the upwardly mobile to make headway. The Church, therefore, lost something in the process, above all its contempt for consequence, a quality which marked the lives of the martyrs. However, this loss was to some extent made up for by the growth within it of the monastic movement, which flourished soon after, even if it did not begin, with the age of Constantine.

The Pre Constantinian Church

The cultural context

The stages by which the infant church articulated the number of its sacred books and its beliefs and groped its way to the discovery of its structures were by no means either clear or neat. Progress may have been faster as far as structures were concerned, in Syria and Asia Minor, a little slower in Alexandria. However, when it came to doctrine and the use of philosophy, Alexandria moved at a more rapid pace than did Rome. It did not proceed by way of organised patterns, but both faith and order arose from pressures applied to it from the outside. The Church was never quite at home in the variety of 'contexts' in which she was born and grew to maturity. She was initially an outcrop of Judaism. But though Christ, his mother and earliest followers were all Jews, the claims made by and for Jesus speedily made them ill at ease among their co-religionists. Believing as they did that Jesus was not only the Messiah of the nation's hopes, but also that he was divine, it is hardly surprising that their fellow countrymen found such beliefs unacceptable. Jesus himself was accused of blasphemy.

Again, Jesus was born into an occupied country. Judea was governed by a Roman governor, Pontius Pilate. The judicial murder of Our Lord and the subsequent refusal of many of the earlier Christians to worship the gods of the state immediately marked them out as 'atheists' and potentially dangerous fanatics, hostile to the government.

Language and thought

Finally the dominant culture of the eastern Mediterranean was Greek. Greek was the '*lingua franca*' of all classes; there had grown up a form of the language known as '*koine*', in use throughout large tracts of the empire. Indeed the liturgy continued to be celebrated in Greek in Rome right up to the time of pope Damasus (366-384). This common language made for speedy and easy communication.

But it also meant that if the gospel was to spread it needed to be translated into a language more readily intelligible than Hebrew. This necessary effort at translation brought with it also the gradual absorption of forms of thought, not naturally at home in Judaea and Palestine. The contrast between these 'modes of thought' can easily be overdrawn. Yet some truth remains in the statement that for the Jews the important question was; 'What shall I do?' while for the Greeks it

was; 'What am I?' Morality is central for the Jew, truth
for the Greek. Christianity was from its outset a
missionary faith; the business of translation therefore
was central. But it was also called on to be faithful to
Jesus and to its roots. This double demand made for
creative tensions at an early stage in the history of the
Church. At times St Paul offered an account of his faith
in language which would have been readily intelligible
to his audience (cf. *Ac* 17:22 ff.). But on other
occasions he stated a strong opposition between the
Gospel and the Greeks (1 *Co* 1:22). Between these two
extremes it was very hard to find a middle way, both
then and now.

The Church and Judaism

The relationship of the Church to its parent Judaism, her
actual position within the Roman Empire and her self-
transformation into a universal faith with the aid of Greek
thought took time. She also needed to keep at bay internal
forces which threatened to disrupt and destroy her very
being. In other words, these early years after the death
and resurrection of Jesus in c. AD 30 were the platform
upon which developed the creeds and structures of the
Church, above all the threefold ministry of bishop, priest
and deacon and her clearly formulated belief in the full
deity of Jesus Christ.

Christian worship

Life in the early church, above all its liturgical practices, is described for us in the early chapters of the Acts of the Apostles. There we learn that the Christians, who thought of themselves as still Jews, met together in the temple for prayers and in their own homes for the breaking of bread. (*Ac* 2:42-46)

Everything was held in common and those in need were helped by the more well off members of the community. All were of one mind and one heart (see *Ac* 4:32 ff). Baptism was administered, sometimes in the name of the Lord Jesus (*Ac* 2:38) but with the progress of time baptism in the threefold name (*Mt* 28:19) became increasingly common. An early second century document known as the *Didache* or *The Teaching of the Twelve Apostles* gave specific instructions, Section 7 reads: "Baptise in the name of the Father and of the Son and of the Holy Spirit, in running water".

The *Didache* also has instructions about the celebration of the Eucharist. But the earliest account of a Sunday Eucharist is provided for us in about 155 by Justin Martyr, who in section 67 of his *First Apology* described what happened, perhaps in order to offset rumours of cannibalistic meals, which had some currency among critics of the 'new religion'. On Sunday the community met under a president, heard passages either from the

writings of the prophets and/or from the memoirs of the
apostles read aloud, (incidentally it is worth noting that
this is the first hint in Christian literature of a liturgical
reading of the Gospels). Then they prayed for their various
needs, and then after the calling down of the Word on the
elements, distributed them both to those present and to
those not there through the ministry of the deacons. We
have to wait till the beginning of the third century for a
more elaborate account of the liturgy from the Apostolic
Tradition of Hippolytus.

First persecutions

During the reign of the Roman emperor Nero (AD 54-68),
we have the first clear account of the persecution of
Christians in about the year AD 65. The Roman historian
Tacitus, in his *Annals* (15,44), speaks of a persecution of
Christians because of their "deadly superstition". Clearly
the emperor was playing on a popular dislike and distrust
of the Christians. Equally clearly Tacitus, although he
wrote in about AD 112, and therefore nearly fifty years
after the death of Nero, in common with the cultured
elite of his day, had little time for Nero himself or
sympathy for Nero's victims. To Tacitus they were "a
class hated for their abominations". Their refusal to 'join
in' and their novelty marked them out as victims of any
state unrest.

Grounds for hostility

Apparently there was at that date no official anti-Christian legislation - that came much later. The popular hostility they caused came from below not from above. Half a century later a Roman governor in Asia Minor, Pliny, wrote in some perplexity to his imperial master, Trajan (98-117), asking what should be done about Christians. The imperial reply is revealing: 'No search should be made for these people; but when they are denounced and found guilty they must be punished' (Pliny, *Letters book* 10, 97). No clear ground for the persecution is given, except that they were 'a contagious and obstinate superstition'. Informants, especially anonymous ones, are discouraged as being 'by no means agreeable to the spirit of the age.'

A further reason for the hostility experienced by many Christians apart from their refusal to join in, was economic. The Council of Jerusalem of AD 45 had forbidden Christians to eat food offered to idols (*Ac* 15:29) and this prohibition, if carried out, presented a threat to the meat markets, whose main sources of meat were the sacrifices offered in pagan temples. It must be admitted that 1 Corinthians 8 rather suggests that some more intellectual Christians disregarded this prohibition. Again, in Ephesus, the Christian opposition to the sale of small silver statues of the virgin goddess, Diana (*Ac* 19:23-40) caused a riot in the city, which echoed to the cry: 'Great is Diana of the Ephesians!'

Ignatius of Antioch

Another 'face' of persecution is provided by the journey to martyrdom and eventual death in Rome at about the same period of Ignatius, bishop of Antioch (c. AD 107). It is hard for us to know exactly why he suffered at all. He may have been betrayed by false friends or enemies in Antioch itself. On his way to Rome he wrote letters to different communities of Christians. Of these, seven survive. They enable us to form some impression of the state of the Church at the beginning of the second century. One of the most striking features is the passionate spirit of love for Jesus and desire for martyrdom. Side by side with that we find him vigorously asserting the true humanity of Jesus, against those who said he only appeared to be human - the so-called Docetists, from the Greek word meaning 'to seem'. What interests us is that it was Christ's humanity rather than the divinity that needed defending.

A further and final feature of these letters is that they speak of the threefold ministry as an already established feature of church life. This means that the Church had at this relatively early date already evolved the structures with which we are today familiar. In the letters of Ignatius there occurs for the first time in any literature the word 'heresy' (*Letter to the Trallians* 6). This was not meant to denote, as it previously had, a particular school of thought, but rather a deviation from the norm of truth, as found in the Catholic church - another expression he was the first to employ (see *Letter to the Smyrneans* 8). This objection to innovation had already been voiced in the New Testament in the Second Letter to Timothy (4:3), where Timothy is warned of the danger of novelties introduced into the gospel for the benefit of those with itching ears.

Old Versus New

About 40 years earlier there had occurred an event of great significance and sadness. In AD 70, Titus, the son of the emperor Vespasian (AD 69-79), and his successor, had taken and sacked Jerusalem. The events so vividly depicted in the gospels (cf. *Mk* 13) had taken place. It meant among other things the end for good of temple sacrifice. It also meant the transportation of the Jews to Jamnia on the sea coast and the growth of an increasingly 'Pharisaic' approach to the nature of Judaism. Some Christians, who up to that date had regarded themselves as both Jews and Christians, could no longer feel that way. It was to encourage such people that the Letter to the Hebrews may have been written.

The sack of Jerusalem marked a new phase in Jewish-Christian relationships. Partly because of growing

intransigence on the Jewish side, expressed in the
'Cursing of the Christians', the Christians themselves, or
some of them, began to question the assumption on which
the New Testament rests, that Christianity is continuous
with Judaism, like a seamless robe. As we have seen, the
early Christians thought of themselves as Jews who
believed that in Jesus of Nazareth, the Messiah of the
nation's hopes had arrived. They continued to use the
temple and the earlier preaching of Saint Paul started at
any rate in the synagogue. (see *Ac* 9:20,13:5 and *Jm* 2:2)

However, even though Paul had insisted on the identity
of the God who created the world and the God who saved
it, between the God of law and the God of grace, Christ
he had written in the first chapter of the Letter to the
Colossians, was both "first born of all creation and first
born from the dead". He had also stressed the novelty of
the gospel he had to preach. Salvation rested not on
works done under the Law, but on the unmerited grace of
Christ (cf. *Rm* 3:28). This emphasis on the novelty of
Christianity over against both Judaism and Hellenism,
especially the former, led Marcion in about AD 140 to
formulate a series of paradoxes in which he contrasted
Old and New, greatly to the disadvantage of the former.
For him the essential message was to be found in the
letters of Paul and in the Gospel of St Luke, suitably
edited, in order to dispose of any favourable references to

creation or to the old order of the Bible. This disposed of the argument from prophecy, on which so much of the gospel of Matthew rests and of the use by the fourth gospel of the identity of the Word through whom the world was made and the Word incarnate in Jesus Christ. There is much to be said for the position of Marcion. There is in many ways quite a gap between the behaviour and demands of God in the two testaments. The vengeful character of the God of the books of Joshua and Judges and some of the psalms, notably 82/83, 108/109 and 136/137, seems a long way from the mercy of Jesus and of his Father. It was not and is not easy to harmonise the two visions. Origen in the third century was in many ways responsible for salvaging the whole bible for the church.

Gnosticism

Marcion's low estimate of the created order was shared by other thinkers of the period, who are often classed together as Gnostics. The word is derived from the Greek word for knowledge, gnosis, so one might possibly translate the word as 'those in the know'. Prominent among the second century Gnostics were two writers, Basilides and Valentinus. Instead of the biblical version of the creation of man, the Gnostics believed that the material universe existed not because God so willed it, as Genesis had taught, but as a result of some great disaster in heaven, which had resulted in the fall of souls from heaven to earth. For the Gnostics the aim of life was the recovery of a lost spiritual paradise.

Gnosis was both a historical movement of uncertain date and origins, and at the same time a way of thinking, a syndrome, as has been argued by Hans Jonas in his *The Gnostic Religion*. Until 1945 all our knowledge of Gnosticism was derived from the hostile accounts of their critics, notably Irenaeus, bishop of Lyons towards the end of the second century. In 1945, however, the picture had to be modified because of the discovery at Nag Hammadi in Upper Egypt of a Gnostic library, now largely housed in the Jung Institute in Zurich. The ideas contained here indicate that the whole movement had a far older origin than the second century AD. Some of them, like the Coptic gospel of Thomas are made up of a series of sayings, purporting to be from Christ and in many respects similar to what we find in the New Testament.

This devaluation of creation and with it much of the Bible forced the Church to clarify her own position. It led her to formulate a positive doctrine of creation, and at the same time not only to insist on the permanent value of the Old Testament, but also to formulate a canon, or list of 'authorised books' in the New Testament. It is not easy to understand why a movement, which stressed the idea that the material world was a sort of cosmic hiccough and which appealed to those who were attracted to what seem to us unusual ideas, should become so popular. We have no knowledge of those who embraced the ideas circulated by Gnosticism, but it is not improbable that the secrecy and philosophical attractiveness of the Gnostic message appealed to those who were themselves more intellectual in their approach to Christianity and therefore felt the need to go beyond the letter of the gospel.

Irenaeus of Lyons

In any event it was clearly perceived as a threat and elicited a large number of responses, all of which insisted on the essential goodness of creation. Prominent among its critics was Irenaeus of Lyons (c. AD 130-200). He came from the Greek East, where he had been a pupil of the aged Polycarp (died AD 156), bishop of Smyrna, who had himself been a disciple of the Apostle John. It is hardly surprising that with such a pedigree behind him, Irenaeus made much of the fact that he could appeal (as presumably the Gnostics could not) to an unbroken succession of teachers and teachings, going right back to the apostles themselves.

Religious truth was not something to be achieved by speculation or by private revelation, but came in a clear and open fashion from the Apostles, above all Peter and Paul and through them to their successors. Irenaeus was the first to formulate a teaching about the apostolic succession of doctrine. Time, history and human beings are the vehicles in and through which the Word of God comes to us.

Against the followers of Valentinus and Basilides he makes a telling point. How can they, he argues, continue to believe in the value of baptism and the importance of eating the body and blood of the Lord in the Eucharist, if matter was of itself intrinsically evil. In a powerful passage in book 5 of his *Against the Heresies* he writes in section 2 'If then the cup of mixed wine and the bread that is made, receives the Word of God and becomes the Eucharist of the body and blood of Christ, how can they deny that the flesh is receptive of the gift of God.'

New Testament Canon

But he also rendered another important service to the Church. It is to him, more than to anyone else, that we owe the present canon of the New Testament of 27 books with its fourfold gospel, Acts and Pauline epistles. However, it is probable that Irenaeus did not invent the canon. The arguments he used for establishing the canon in book 3 of *Against the Heresies* are so strange that it looks as though he was defending a position that was already by and large accepted. The fact that there are four beasts in the book of Revelation or four principal winds or four pillars of the universe seems to us hardly persuasive arguments. It is true that the Church had to wait till 367 for Athanasius (297-373) to formulate the 27 books of the New Testament, but it is worthwhile remembering that the Church pre-existed the New Testament and also that the Church decided what belonged to it.

Apologists for the Church

The second century was an important and exciting time for the young Church. In addition to the fight to articulate her position vis-à-vis Judaism and Gnosticism, and face sporadic persecution from the Romans, she began to 'meet' the Greek world. There are indeed evidences of the encounter with the Greeks in the New Testament, above all in the fourth Gospel (cf. *Jn* 12:20), where the Greeks come to Philip and say "Sir, we should like to see Jesus". Reference has already been made to the meeting on the Areopagus between Paul and the Greek philosophers. But by and large the New Testament is written "from faith to faith". By the middle of the next century the Church had expanded well beyond the limits of Palestine and the Synagogue. The ends of the known world were the limit (cf. *Ac* 1:8). St Paul's expressed intention was to pass through Rome "on his way to Spain" (*Rm* 15:28).

It became imperative for the missionary Church to develop a new and if possible coherent strategy with which to deal with the problems of evangelisation and the attacks on the young Church. Above all she was accused of atheism, cannibalism and incest. Atheism for her refusal to worship the traditional gods of Rome;

cannibalism, because of a very natural misunderstanding of the Eucharist; incest, perhaps because the new converts called each other 'brother' and 'sister' and were also married. Faced with such criticism it was hardly possible to remain silent. It became necessary for her to defend herself and we find in this period a large number of *Apologies*, especially designed to deal with such attacks, and at the same time, on a more positive note, to offer to the pagan world reasons for giving the gospel a hearing.

The genre of apology was not strictly speaking new. Plato had composed an apology for his master Socrates, defending him against the charge of corrupting the young and of teaching atheism. Again, the speech of Saint Paul on the Areopagus, recorded at Acts 17 was a not entirely successful attempt, to recommend the gospel to the cultured despisers of the new religion.

Justin Martyr

Prominent among these Apologists was Justin Martyr (c. AD 100-165). He came from Sychar (modern Nablus) in Samaria. Unlike many of his predecessors he came to Christianity through the door of Greek philosophy, and even after his conversion he continued to regard his faith as 'the true philosophy' and to wear the black robe of the professional philosopher - a sort of university gown or monastic habit. One of his principal aims was to take over as much philosophy as he could and 'baptise' it. This he did because he thought that there was a basic harmony between the teachings of Socrates and Christ. Indeed for him Socrates was a 'Christian before Christ' (cf. *1st Apology* 1.46). According to Justin we all share the same seeds of the Word, of which Christ is the fullest and most perfect expression. In general terms the aim of Justin was twofold; i) to argue that there was no necessary connection between Greek religion and Greek philosophy and ii) to effect a marriage between Greek philosophy and the gospel. This dual motive was not likely to recommend itself to supporters of the old pagan ways. This resentment found expression in *The True Account of Celsus* written in about 173 not long after Justin's death in Rome in 165/166. It was to refute the critique of the gospel of Christ as an irrational religion designed for women and people of subnormal intelligence, that Origen in about 250 composed his eight volume work entitled *Against Celsus*. It was the contention of Celsus and of his successors that Greek culture formed an undivided and indivisible unity and therefore it was not possible to have the philosophy and culture and reject the religion.

The Church in North Africa

It is difficult to date with precision the arrival of the gospel in North Africa. The fact that the martyrdom of Perpetua and Felicity occurred in AD 202 suggests that it was already flourishing at least as early as the last third of the second century. It is to the church in North Africa that we owe the earliest Latin version of the New Testament, known as the *Vetus latina*. But the great moment in the history of the church in North Africa was the conversion of Tertullian in about the year 195. He was probably a lawyer, though almost certainly not a priest. Justin and Origen's philosophic and generous approach to the relation between Christ and culture was not shared by him or by many other Christians. Tertullian (c.160-225) in particular preferred to stress the difference between Christ and Plato. In chapter 46 of his *Apologeticus*, written in 197, he asks the question "But then, what have philosopher and Christian in common...the thief of truth and its guardian?" To this question, the implied though not the stated, answer is 'nothing whatever!' Tertullian appealed above all to those passages in 1 Corinthians, where St Paul also had insisted on the radical difference between faith and philosophy. In another work *On the*

Flesh of Christ (5) he defends his position and belief with the famous and often misquoted aphorism; "I believe because it is strange" (not as usually quoted 'absurd').

Yet despite this confrontational approach we find Tertullian referring to the Stoic philosopher Seneca, who also died in AD 65 at the instance of his old pupil Nero, being referred to by Tertullian as "our Seneca". Again, perversely enough, it was to Tertullian above all that the Western Church owed the creation of a theological vocabulary, with the use of words like 'person' and 'substance' expressions that found their way into the formula of Pope Leo the Great in his letter to the Council of Chalcedon (451) but introduced into the theological vocabulary of his day in his treatise, *Against Praxeas*.

Further Persecution

The death of Tertullian about 220 did not mean the end of Christianity in North Africa. In about 246 Cyprian a pagan rhetorician was converted to Christ and within two years he was elected bishop of Carthage. He suffered martyrdom there on 14th September 258 during the persecution of Valerian. Although he is reported by Jerome (c. 340-420) to have been in the habit of saying, 'Hand me down the master' by which he meant Tertullian, he did not share the 'zealous fanaticism' of his master. Tertullian ended his days as a Montanist, an ecstatic sect with its roots in central Turkey, and as a result withdrew from the main body of the church, Cyprian's main claim to fame is his treatment of those who lapsed in the time of persecution and his treatise *On the Unity of the Church*.

In the year 202 there broke out a severe persecution against the Christians under the emperor Septimius Severus. It was the first of several attacks on the Church, which reached their climax under Diocletian in 303. The motives for these outbursts are by no means clear. What does seem certain is that they were engineered from the top downward, unlike the popular agitation we have seen before under Nero and Trajan. Looked at afterwards it seems to us rather like the dying spasm of a dead or dying monster. But this is hindsight. It is hard also to discover with what intensity the attack was conducted, with what success and how many actual martyrs there were.

Martyrs

In the persecution of 202 there perished at Carthage two female martyrs, Perpetua and Felicity. A moving and near contemporary account of their deaths, perhaps composed by Tertullian shortly afterwards, survives. As with Ignatius of Antioch, about 100 years earlier it is possible to detect something of the enthusiasm with which they approached their death. Perpetua was of noble birth, Felicity was a slave, yet they were united in their devotion to their faith. They met their deaths after several visions in the arena at Carthage on 7th March 203 through the attack of a caged leopard.

It was in the same persecution that Origen nearly lost his life at the age of seventeen, prevented only from joining his father, Leonidas, by the action of his mother in hiding his cloths It was in the same persecution that Clement of Alexandria saved his life by flight to Palestine. He is said to have justified his flight by using the words of Christ in Matthew 10:23, 'If they persecute you in one town flee to another'. Later on in the same century, nearly 50 years later in the persecution of Decius (250/1) Origen, much to his regret, suffered torture but survived. This persecution arose from the emperor's desire to celebrate the millennium of the foundation of the city of Rome by Romulus and Remus.

Denial under persecution

The exceptional fierceness of the persecution of Decius in 250 had caused many to lapse either by actually sacrificing to the pagan gods, or by handing over the sacred books, or what amounted to the same in the eyes of their critics, what had the appearance of being sacred books. This put the church into a difficult position. What should she do with such as had denied their faith? Should they be readmitted and if so on what terms? They clamoured to be allowed back, but not unnaturally, those who had borne the heat and burden of the day resented this.

Cyprian, bishop of Carthage from 248 till 258, tried to resolve the issue by requiring a lengthy penance which might extend over a number of years. Writing in the middle of the third century in his *On the Lapsed*, Cyprian takes rather a severe view, though in the end he inclines to leniency. Those readmitted to communion must "beg and pray assiduously, spend the day sorrowing and the night in vigils and tears" (section 35). Others, above all in North Africa, 'the church of the martyrs' with a pedigree stretching back to the Maccabees, were more severe even than Cyprian. The Donatists, who had remained faithful throughout the persecutions refused to recognize the validity of sacraments celebrated by those who had apostatized, claimed Cyprian as their patron and continued until well after the death of their founding fathers. Indeed, though condemned by a conference held in Carthage in 411 they carried on until they were swept away by the Arab invasions of the seventh and eighth centuries.

The whole schism raised the vital question about the nature and meaning of the holiness of the church. Did it derive primarily from the moral excellence of its members or from the holiness of its head, that is Christ? The Donatist church in North Africa proper arose from the problem posed by the strength of some and the laxity of others. The Melitian schism in Egypt (c.306) rose at

about the same time for similar reasons. Both of these
groups thought the terms for the readmission of the
lapsed during the persecution of the Emperor Diocletian
far too lax.

Refusal to conform

The underlying motive for the third century AD
persecutions seems to have been less the actual beliefs of
the Christians than the threat which their refusal to
conform at least outwardly posed to the well being of
society. Good citizenship was linked to the worship of the
gods of society and even more to the reverence for the
emperor demanded of all citizens, especially soldiers. In
other words refusal to conform at least outwardly was
regarded then and later as a form of treason. The seeds of
subsequent tensions within the church were already sown
during its first 300 years, above all the relation between
religion and society. It has not yet gone away as the present
pope's address in Regensburg in 2006 has demonstrated.

The Church and Culture

At the same time as these persecutions occurred another movement was taking place in Alexandria, of a very different kind. Ever since its foundation by Alexander the Great in 331 BC, Alexandria had been a wealthy, cosmopolitan city with a famous library and university. It also possessed a very high proportion of Jewish settlers, who occupied two quarters of the city. Here perhaps more than anywhere else arose the problem of what might be called 'inculturation'. What ought to be the relation of Jews and Christians to the surrounding culture?

Towards the middle of the third century BC the Jews produced the Greek version of the Old Testament, known as the *Septuagint*, (referred to with the Roman numerals LXX) probably at the suggestion of Ptolemy Philadelphus (285-246). At a later date appeared the books of Wisdom and Ecclesiasticus, which display considerable Hellenistic influence. In Alexandria at any rate, and probably, though to a lesser extent in Palestine there existed a fusion of biblical and external learning. The book of Wisdom dated to the end of the second or beginning of the first century BC almost certainly exercised considerable influence on the letters of Paul to the Romans and Ephesians.

Later than that a Jew, Philo, (circa 25 BC - AD 40) had
tried to show the harmony between the Bible and the
learning of the Greeks by producing a vast commentary
on the book of Genesis. In this he used a method of
expounding the scriptures known as allegory. This
method of treating any sacred text had already been
applied by Heraclitus in the second century BC to the text
of Homer. It was assumed by him (and by his later
Christian imitators) that beneath the normal, historical
sense of the inspired text there existed another, deeper
meaning, of either a moral or metaphysical character. We
can find traces of this method in the New Testament in
the allegory of the vine in John 15 and in St Paul's
treatment of the Old Testament in 1 Corinthians 10:11.

This whole cultural milieu found a ready welcome
among a section of the Christians though not among all.
Prominent among the inculturators was Clement of
Alexandria, an Athenian convert to the Gospel in the last
third of the second century, or slightly earlier. His main
surviving writings, *Protrepticus* or *Encouragement to
Philosophy*, *Paedagogus* or *Schoolmaster*, and *Stromateis*
or *Miscellanies* are full of Greek culture. He was
determined to show that there was a place for culture
within the Church. Though insisting on the superiority of
his faith to that of philosophy, he also insisted on the
continuity of secular culture with that of the Word of

God. Both the Old Testament and Greek philosophy were treated as schoolmasters leading men to the gospel of Christ. He also wrote a short work entitled, *What rich man shall be saved?* It is in effect an attempt to take the sting out of Christ's charge to the rich young man, recorded at Mark 10:17-27. Part, at any rate, of Clement's purpose there and elsewhere was to show that Christianity did not require either absolute indigence on the part of Christians or absence of intelligence. He can be understood therefore as offering an orthodox response to the challenge of Gnosticism, by trying to find a place within the official church for those who might otherwise have found it too lacking in intellectual challenge to satisfy them.

Origen

In comparison with Clement, his successor Origen (185-254) was a giant. He was the first to attempt a systematic account of the Christian faith in his great dogmatic work *On First Principles*, completed some time before he was forced to leave Alexandria for Caesarea in Palestine in AD 231/2. He offered his system as a tribute to those who were willing to go with him beyond the first articles of faith and to search for their mutual coherence and philosophic basis, to pass from faith to understanding. In the beginning of this four volume work he discusses the nature of God and distances himself from all those who possess a crude human, materialist picture of God. With no one more than Origen is the whole aim to 'demythologise' the common pictures we have of God. God for Origen is very much like the account given of him in the first of the *39 Articles*[1], he has neither body, parts nor passions. He is also to be thought of as embodying four important qualities: power, wisdom, justice and goodness. Having purified our image of God we are left with the idea of a pure, simple intellect, both creator and eternal Father of the Son, who is eternally generated by him. In this highly abstract system we can already discern the seeds of the creed of Nicaea of a century later, with its insistence on the eternal generation of the Son.

Origen's wide contribution

Systematic theology was by no means the sole contribution made by Origen to the thinking of the Church. Towards the end of *On first Principles*, Origen provides an account of the way to deal with just those

---

[1] "…There is but one living and true God, everlasting, without body, parts, or passions; of infinite power, wisdom, and goodness; the Maker, and Preserver of all things both visible and invisible. And in unity of this Godhead there be three Persons, of one substance, power, and eternity; the Father, the Son, and the Holy Ghost."

'awkward' passages in the Old (and New) Testaments, out
of which Marcion had constructed his case. It is hardly
surprising to find him advocating allegory and invoking
the authority of St Paul for doing so; 1 Corinthians 9:9
and 10:1 ff. and Galatians 4:24, where the word allegory
is actually used. There Paul uses allegory in order to
interpret Old Testament sayings.

In another area also, Origen had great influence. He
insisted, against the Gnostics, on the vital importance of
freedom as the condition of the possibility of virtue. Against
the Montanists - a group originating in c. AD 173 in central
Turkey, who laid great stress on the importance of ecstasy -
Origen argued that the presence of the Holy Spirit was
always peaceful and full of light (cf. *On first Principles*
3.3.4). This dual insistence on freedom and the mind as of
the first importance in the Christian life had a very powerful
influence on subsequent spirituality. Origen's vision is one
of light and liberty; he has no room for 'enthusiasm' on the
one hand or for passivity on the other.

Not only did Origen provide later generations with a
useful scheme for interpreting scripture; he also composed
a series of homilies and commentaries on all the books of
the Old and most of those of the New Testament. In these
we are able to glimpse the ardent student turned pastor at
work. He is able to turn the most unpromising passages
from Joshua and Leviticus into spiritual fruit. In them we

occasionally see something of the personal devotion of Origen to Jesus combined with a less rigid adherence to the principles of theology enunciated in his more overtly theological writings. In this two-sidedness he has something in common with his only real rival in the Early Church - Augustine of Hippo (354-430).

Origen was forced to leave Alexandria in 231 and spent the rest of his life at Caesarea in Palestine. There he composed his great eight volume work (mentioned above) *Against Celsus*. In the course of this writing he endeavoured to deal with the first important reply to the whole Christian enterprise, written by Celsus in about 173 AD. The central thrust of Celsus' work is that Christianity is a religion for women and simple people and that any attempt to adorn it with the dress of reason is misconceived. Origen replies that the gospel is for all, not simply for the clever, but it is also for the clever (1,9). He is happy to borrow from the Greeks and will on occasion employ what he calls common ideas or notions, that is universal ideas (1,4) of which everyone has a share, simply in virtue if being human. Punishment for Origen is largely corrective (4,10) and in this he agrees with and perhaps depends upon the *Gorgias* of Plato. In reply to the indictment of Christianity as a new religion and therefore that it could not be true he replies at 1,26 that it is as old as Judaism if not older.

A Growing Church

As early as the death of Origen in 254, Christianity had made astonishing advances from its humble and obscure beginnings in Palestine. It could now number communities right round the shores of the Mediterranean. As we have already seen, the Gospel had arrived in Britain well before the beginning of the fourth century, at least three hundred years before the arrival of Augustine in Kent in 597. It had by then, in 254, its sacred books, its ordered hierarchy, a developing theology, a glorious record of martyrs and a defined position over against Greeks and Jews alike.

Rome and monasticism

Two further growths on the soil of the Gospel also occurred at about this time. i) A growing awareness of the importance of the bishop of Rome, ii) the beginning of the monastic movement:

i) As capital of the empire it was quite natural that the church in Rome should come to take precedence over other churches. Over and above this political reason we can see her pre-eminence being connected at an early date with the deaths at Rome of the great apostles Peter and Paul during the persecution of Nero in AD 67. It was not therefore simply (or indeed primarily) to the Roman empire that the bishops of Rome owed their primacy but to the blood of the apostles, above all Peter. In support of this claim in about 256 we find Stephen, the bishop of Rome, appealing to Matthew 16:18, 'Thou art Peter', in defence of his prerogatives against Cyprian of Carthage (cf. Cyprian, *On the Unity of the Church* 4 - a much disputed and very important passage in the whole debate about the primacy of the see of Rome).

ii) At about the same time a movement of a very different kind was taking place in Egypt. In 270 a young man, Antony, heard in church the words of Christ to the rich young man, "Go, sell what you have, give to the poor and come follow me" (*Mt* 19:21). So moved was he that having sold his property and provided for his sister he withdrew into the desert by progressive stages in search of God. This action of his is regarded as the beginning of the monastic movement, which gathered force under Constantine and his sons and spread well beyond Egypt. Its success was due to two factors; it was helped by the increased involvement of the Church in the world, resulting from the conversion of Constantine. But it also drew strength at a slightly later date from the immensely popular Life of Antony written by St Athanasius in c. 356.

Schism and Heresy

The last full-scale persecution of the Church came to an end in 311 with the Edict of Toleration and a year later with the conversion of Constantine. Naturally enough the emperor regarded the Church as bound to him by special ties and he came to think of the relation of Church and state not unlike the way his predecessors had thought of that of state and religion. An ordered peaceful Church was the guarantee of an ordered peaceful empire. Unfortunately for this vision there existed then in the Church elements that threatened this harmony, Donatism and Arianism.

Donatus

Donatus and his followers took the view that to have fallen from Christianity during the great persecution of Diocletian was not only gravely sinful, but also disqualified those who had done so from membership of the Church and (if they were priests) from the power to administer valid sacraments. This extreme position led to a schism in the North African church in 311 with the elevation to the see of Carthage of Caecilian. Not only had he as archdeacon failed to give the martyrs due reverence; he had also been consecrated by Felix, bishop of Aptunga, who was (wrongly, as it turned out) accused of having surrendered the sacred books in the persecution. This schism the emperor tried (without much success) to mend. A synod held in Arles in 314 decided against Donatus, but this did not terminate the schism, which rent N. Africa in half for the next century till 411.

Arius

Constantine's intervention on the more purely dogmatic front was hardly more successful. In about AD 319 Arius, a presbyter of Alexandria, had caused alarm and division by affirming that Christ was not fully divine. He was a creature 'but not as one of the creatures'. Arius' popularity (and potential danger) may have arisen from his attempt to popularise his views by means of verses to be sung 'on the sea, on the road and at the mill'. Such a view was in some respects conservative and could appeal to certain texts in scripture, like Proverbs 8:22 "The Lord created me in the beginning of his days (Wisdom is speaking)" and Colossians 1:15, Christ is 'the first born of all creation' which treated the son as a creature.

Council of Nicaea

However it failed to do justice either to popular piety or to the basic understanding of Christ's person and mission as redeemer, which had been current since the gospel and Ignatius of Antioch. In order, therefore, to restore some measure of harmony to the Church the emperor took the unprecedented step of summoning a council of some 220 bishops in May 325. It met at Nicaea and besides condemning Arius it also produced the Nicene Creed. This creed, which is the basis of the eucharistic creed, affirmed that the Son was 'consubstantial with the Father, God from God, light from light'. Two bishops resisted the imperial pressure to sign and were exiled. Apparently peace was restored. But under the sons and successors of Constantine this peace was illusory and short-lived. Fifty years of infighting followed and at one point it looked as though the party condemned at Nicaea might be reinstated. The emperors found to their cost that it was less easy than they might have thought to treat the Church as part of their highly efficient civil service. Unlike the religious leaders of the pagan religious systems, the Christians were not prepared to set aside their religious convictions to satisfy the demands of a Christian emperor.

The Emergence of Orthodoxy

One of the important truths which emerges from the above account is that the church of the pre-Constantinian era was by no means monochrome. From very early days there existed quite substantial differences of opinion on serious issues. The struggle with Marcion had the double effect of defending the place and value of the Old Testament within the church and at the same time of helping to establish the canon of the New Testament of 27 books. It had also helped the church to articulate and defend the search for meanings other than the merely literal. The challenge of Gnosticism helped the church to recognise and defend the importance of the created order and at the same time insist on the importance of freedom against what seemed like a doctrine of predestination. The encounter with the non Jewish world encouraged men like Justin and Tertullian to explore the relationship between faith and reason, between Christianity and philosophy, a problem which is just as challenging now as it was in the second century AD. This challenge is also evident in the writings of Origen, who endeavoured to explore the underlying structure of the creed. Finally, one of the central ways in which men like Irenaeus endeavoured to deal with the fissiparous tendencies of Gnosticism was an appeal both to tradition and authority with in the church. He was helped in his endeavour by the prior existence within the church of structures of authority, above all the three fold ministry already clearly articulated in the seven letters of Ignatius to the churches of Asia Minor.

Uniformity and flexibility

Did this gradual process mean a change in Christianity, as it lost or seemed to lose its pluriformity and acquired what might be termed a straight jacket? Did it begin life as a democracy and then find itself under Episcopal/papal control? Did she thus lose with the progress of time a variety and, as it were a symphonic character only to be replaced by a monochrome type of uniformity? One thing that can certainly be said is that although certain areas, like authority and dogma acquired a certain degree of uniformity, this by no means constricted the church. Some issues may have been solved, but others arose to take their place, as the history of the councils makes very clear. Again, even the areas where a certain uniformity arose by no means excluded further exploration. Even after the decisions of Nicaea had been taken, the dispute still went on about how the unity and Trinity of God were to be understood and most of these issues had already been voiced well before 325. Again the arguments surrounding the place and nature of the humanity of Christ did not depart, despite the efforts of Ignatius and Irenaeus.

Conclusion

The first 300 years of the history of the Church are quite remarkable, above all if we compare the humble, provincial beginnings with the spread, structure, creed and influence she possessed in 337. But, though it is possible to outline the main stages and areas of expansion, it is much less easy to account for them on purely historical grounds. Imperial favour may help to explain the later spread of the Gospel, but not what happened prior to 313. Nor is it fair to argue that paganism was on its last legs and that Christianity filled the gap left by it. Doubtless various elements combined to produce the final effect. Christianity did offer a better hope to a weary world than many of its rivals. It also demanded from its adherents a change of life. The courage of Christians during persecution and their care for the poor and the widows clearly made a deep impression. Its basic assertion "Jesus is LORD" (1 Co 12:3) was at the root of its faith and the continuous guidance of the Holy Spirit begun at the first Pentecost (Ac 2) did the rest.

How self evident was it that what actually emerged at the end of the period of repression and actual persecution should have been what it turned out to be?

The early church was by no means a monolith. It was in some respects more various than it came to be, though even after 313 variety was very evident. Tensions existed in many areas: Montanism raised the question of the place of prophecy and ecstasy within the church, while at the same time questioning the increasing place of rationalism within the church. Gnosticism offered a home in the church to people of wealth and intelligence, who while they might have felt excluded themselves came to be perceived themselves as a divisive and exclusive force. Yet neither Montanism nor Gnosticism 'died' despite the opposition they provoked. Some of the insights of both were taken over by the majority church. The place of non rational experiences within the church was taken over by the later Messalian movement and Clement of Alexandria distinguished between true and false Gnosis. In the middle years of the third century a latter day variant of Gnosticism was inspired by the writings of a Persian Christian named Mani (216-276). He fell foul of both of the imperial authorities and the bishops and was finally executed in 276. But the dualistic position which he advocated did not die with him and was, as it were, taken up by the Bogomils in the Balkans in the 11th century and the Cathars in southern France slightly later.

Faith and reason

Docetism, by denying the reality of Christ's humanity and Sabellianism, which denied any important distinction between the three persons of the Trinity, also helped to enrich and complicate the picture. All these movements, which came to be seen as heretical did not begin life with the intention of introducing novelties or as breaking from some already existent pattern. But, as with Montanism and Gnosticism so too the problems raised about the reality of Christ's humanity and the relation between the unity and Trinity of God are still with us. Finally and most importantly the relation between faith and secular reason was never solved and still remains with us. The contrasting positions of Justin and Tertullian still exist within the Christian church.

How many Christians were there at the end of the period under review? This is not an easy question to answer. Edward Gibbon in his *Decline and Fall of the Roman Empire* argued that in 251 there were something in the region of 50,000 Christians in Rome itself, about 5 per cent out of a population of around a million. But other writers think this too high a proportion. The numbers in the east were probably much higher and by the time Constantine arrived at the gates of Rome, perhaps as much as a tenth of the population had embraced the 'new' religion in the west, rather more in the east. In any event this means that his conversion is unlikely to have taken place on purely political grounds.

Literature

One further feature of the first 300 years of the spread of
the gospel is the amazing literary activity above all if we
compare it with what came from non Christian writers.
With the exception of the *Handbook* of Alcinous and the
Meditations of the emperor, Marcus Aurelius in the second
and the *Enneads* of Plotinus in the third century there is
little else. At the same time the beleaguered Christians
produced Justin, Irenaeus, Tertullian, Cyprian, Clement of
Alexandria and above all the stupendous genius of Origen.
As Robin Lane Fox observes on page 335 of his *Pagans
and Christians*, "In cities of growing social divisions,
Christianity offered unworldly equality. It preached and at
its best practised love in a world of widespread brutality. It
offered certainty and won conviction, where the great
venture of Greek philosophy, was widely perceived to have
argued itself into the ground".

Influence of Paul

How it came to pass that orthodoxy, or what came to be
thought of as orthodoxy eventually asserted itself is not at
all clear. Perhaps the most important tangible feature is the
historical sense of the early Christian writers, above all
saint Paul, who saw in the historical events of the life of
Jesus, above all his death and resurrection 'according to
the scriptures' (1 *Co* 15:3) the ultimate justification of and

for their religion. They were all convinced of the importance of history and of visible continuity with the past. This sense of a necessary continuity with the past lies behind much of what Irenaeus and Origen had to offer.

Again how was the evident diversity within the church related to the growth of orthodoxy? If one compares the state of the church in 30 with that in 330 there are obvious differences. Her members were no longer largely Jewish, nor were they drawn almost entirely from the poorer members of society. Some doubtless lamented the changes and looked back to the early years, others realised that the way forward lay in dialogue with the surrounding society All these approaches had their attendant challenges. Neither the literal sense of scripture by itself, nor a liberal dialogue with the world around was by itself enough. Christianity was neither a watered down form of Judaism, nor Greek wisdom in the clothing of Christian language. It was a fusion of both, inspired by one person, Jesus Christ of Nazareth, true God and true man.